What People Are Saying

Dear Radomir,

This is the simplest, most enlightening book I've ever read. I would go as far as stating this book beats any bible out in the world. Not that I'm religious, but I'd stack it up there. I've looked through many self-help books. By the time I finish 100-200 pages of crap, I've lost myself in what specific help I was looking for. I'm a new husband with a uncompassionate non-empathetic wife and the cutest 2 year old. I've been married 3 years. I love her and my child because love has reserved a place in my heart for better or worse. I'm seeing a psychiatrist for my troubled marriage. They don't seem to cure what's really ailing me, which is the heartache of love. In one week's time your wisdom has turned the tides of my failing marriage. I have empowered myself as a confident male and followed your 14 pages of pure sweet knowledge. My wife is now calling and wanting to sweet talk and she's listening to my new-found rules I've laid down for myself. In a way, your book is all about helping me and through that is a byproduct of a happy wife. Its working so well . . . . I just might keep it a secret for awhile, but it will work for the ladies too.

Please feel free to use me as a reference for doubting husbands in the USA. No buddy can truly believe the wisdom in your book unless he/she reads it and all in one night which is awesome. A personal note to all the husbands suffering in America and elsewhere: This book is universally true that works to win your love back.

Kind Regards,

William J.Memphis, TN

Dear Mr. Samardzic,

I can hardly believe what a change the manual has made in my life. It is like I am a new person. My relationship with the man I love is completely new, and he is much happier. We talk openly about things that used to be painful. I pass places on the street where we used to meet, and whereas before I would be sad to see them, lamenting times gone by, now I am unaffected and just smile at the memory.

But the remarkable thing to me is that other areas of my life are so much better. I have to fly all the time for my job, and suddenly I am no longer afraid to fly. I used to have panic attacks and they are gone. I'm a little afraid to wake up from this dream, because it seems too good to be true in a way. But the great thing is that, instead of worrying like I used to about whether he will be in my life in the future, I am free to imagine a great life for myself. I hope he will want to share it, but it will be great with or without him.

Oh, one more interesting thing is that some of my friends are frustrated because I don't talk about him to them any more like I used to. It makes me realize that much of our relationship consisted of complaining about the men in our lives. I have no interest in it anymore.

So, this is all to say that I can't believe what a difference you have made in my life. I used to see other people in relationships and think, what class did I miss in school that everyone else had but I missed, so I don't get to have relationships like that? Now, I have had my class! And the best part is that I am no longer jealous of other people being in committed relationships.

I feel freed from years of misery.

Thanks, thanks, thanks.

Monica A.
Saint Louis, MO

"Thank you for helping to put an end to an emotionally abusive relationship. I realized with your help that the most important relationship in need of repair was the relationship I was having with myself."

Debby K
Dallas, TX

"There is something to be said for the theory of "cause and affect." Changing what I was doing in my relationship actually changed my partner's actions as well. Our relationship of 16 years did NOT end because of the valuable information I received from the "Relationship Saver". If your relationship is in trouble, I urge you to try it and learn about new and greater possibilities for a more loving and happy partnership."

Andrea M.
Los Angeles, CA

I stumbled upon your book when I was groping in darkness with the reality that my marriage had hit a path of no return. My central problem was kind of spiritual—"nobody in this world understands me!" I had knocked on almost all the doors and none opened to me! Then I saw your web site and the content was so compelling and genuine that I decided to buy the manual.

It indeed created a magic. How well you have condensed the whole secret of human relationship in just 14 pages!

Very glad to say that I have won my family back, and we have relocated to Cupertino, CA from Bangalore, India.

Indeed, I have no words to express my gratitude. I pray that your message continues to save more and more families.

Thank you very much.

A. Ramesh
Cupertino, CA

Radomir,

I purchased your book and am amazed at the things I've taken for granted and the things I've never thought of before!! Thank you for opening my eyes to this new insight.

I have read the book through once and plan to read it every day and apply it to my life and to our relationship.

Thank-you! Thank-you very much!

This IS the way. By being truthfully honest and seeing it from HER point of view.

Now, I need to get on with building a life, and if she wants to be part of it, THEN we can build a marriage.

Thank-you Sir. One day you will REAP your reward.

Dear Radomir,

Thank you ever so much for your intelligent manual. The worst crisis I ever lived is perfectly solved following your unique instructions of talking only about the future. My husband had left our home, he had no communication with me for a month, behaved to our son and myself as if we were divorced, and sent me official divorce papers. Nevertheless, I trusted everything was apparent. That is when I discovered you manual. We had three talks, each of which I carried out following your instructions. After the first one (and the divorce papers) divorcing was no point, and communication improved. The second and third talks were on a trip he invited me to, properly as a stranger, having been away from home one and a half months. During and after the trip he gained peace and confidence, we got closer, and had a daily good communication, though he did not come back to our house.

Three months after leaving he came back, and we are having a wonderful time. Thanks God, not only did you teach me how to solve that terrible crisis, but also how to avoid such situations for good. God bless you, dearest counselor. You manual is most valuable.

Knowing how busy you are this is a brief message. If any additional information might be useful for you, I would be glad to provide it. If you want to publish it, I would rather have you change my real name, for my husband is a well know writer, and our marriage is an example of harmony!

My best regards, good soul.

Good day Radomir,

Thanks for your book. Since reading your book, my wife has torn up the divorce papers . . .

We are both starting to appreciate each others company and are looking forward to moving back together later this year. Thanks again for the simple and easy to follow ideas in your book.

Regards,

Russell. B,Australia

Hi,

I purchased your book and read it today! I am amazed at the insight I received and how I had been doing things so wrong.

Denise V. USA

Again, you are so right. I have read the book three times now. Each time I get more out of it.

Yesterday I was crying. Today I am smiling.

Tomorrow I will laugh out loud. And I will read it again tomorrow. And the next day . . . .

Many thanks,

Arline UK

Dear Radomir Samardzic,

After several months I tried again, and everything worked like a charm. A first glance through the book gave me an immediately positive reaction.

Although your suggestions seem counter-intuitive to one's normal reactions, they make a great deal of sense to me now, based on my own experience in the meantime.

Thank you.

Christopher A. UK

If you want a better relationship NOW . . . . this is the book for you!

"The Gameless Relationship" sets forth, in a quick, clear, and extremely understandable way, exactly what you can do today to make your relationship dream come true, right now! All you need is a bit of willingness to follow the exercises and start having that gameless relationship today. You will learn that you have 100% control over what you get!

As a business management seminar presenter and corporate coach for over 25 years, many books have crossed my desk. I find "The Gameless Relationship" to be one of the best at explaining exactly what it takes to have a gameless, loving relationship. And, a bonus is that the self-awareness and skills you find here will carry you through all of your relationships, personal and professional.

"The Gameless Relationship" is short, clear and laser-focused on exactly what you need to do to have your dream loving relationship as well as happier, more fun relationships in your life.

Barbara A. Clegg, MS, RCC
Clegg Coaching & Training LLC
Los Angeles 04/2009

Dear Mr. Samardzic,

Thank you for this great book (The Gameless Relationship). It made our relationship as solid as a rock. We love it.

It is the most complete relationship book that I've seen. It is short, but it relies on principles that you can apply to any situation. You can read thousands of pages of hows and whys in other books, but this one beats them all. Brilliant!

Thank you.

Bob and Sandy
Massachusetts
USA

The Relationship Bible

The Relationship Bible

*A Definitive Manual for Saving
and Creating Successful Relationships
and Marriages*

Radomir Samardzic

To order additional copies of this book, contact:
Xlibris Corporation
1-888-795-4274
www.Xlibris.com
Orders@Xlibris.com
31850

CONTENTS

FOREWORD

This book consists of two, at first sight, very different parts that initially appeared in e-book format. Part One is completely dedicated to saving and improving your relationships. It is written in a manual format and is meant to help you learn how to repair and improve your relationships in the shortest possible time. It'll take you only fifteen to twenty minutes to read—no fluff, no stories, only straight-to-the-point instructions.

If you are to save your relationship, I encourage you to read Part One MANY times and USE it. Behind seemingly simple and straightforward instructions there is a lot of psychology, experience and testing involved. Even many spiritual teachings are represented.

As of this writing, Part One, as a separate book, has sold over 35,000 copies.

Part Two is meant to be used after you have repaired your relationship, or if your relationship does not need fixing or repair. It deals with four basic principles of a relationship where playing games is redundant. Although it has only four basic principles, it encompasses all nuances and variations on the same theme. It goes much more in depth than Part One, although it is also concise and without stories, examples and such, for the sake of keeping it simple and to the point.

Many people said this book should be used in schools and businesses and I hope that one day it will. In the meantime, it is my pleasure and privilege to offer it to people like you with the hope that your relationships may take a quantum leap for the better and in so doing leave a positive mark on humanity in general.

Note: Although I sometimes address him and sometimes her, this book applies to both genders equally.

Thank you.

Radomir Samardzic

PART ONE

The Relationship Saver

Fast track manual for relationship saving and/or repair

*"We can't solve problems by
using the same kind of thinking we used
when we created them."*

Albert Einstein

INTRODUCTION

Many of this manual's instructions may be contrary to *your* logical thinking and instinctual reaction.

Also please take note: Nothing that you read in the following pages is TRUE, per se, but if you apply it, it will turn your relationship around. The choice is yours.

Humans are not logical creatures when it comes to relationships.

We are "feeling" creatures for most of the time. A great majority of our decisions are based on our feelings. (Think, for example, about how you make decisions when you are either upset, afraid or madly in love?) In the long run, those successful relationships are the ones that are based on "thinking;" "feeling" relationships are eventually doomed to failure, i.e., you are bound to fall out of love at some point. I am not saying that one should have no feelings, but a *basis for building a successful relationship cannot rely solely on feelings.*

To make things even worse, we are born into a world where there is no training ground for relationships. Our educational system does not have 'relationship classes.' We are thrown into relationships practically from the beginning of our lives. Thereafter, *life consistently comes at us with all these relationships and no one really knows, nor can anyone tell us, how to make them work or improve them.*

This manual is a simple guide for repairing your relationship, that is if you really want to have a healthy, loving and satisfying relationship and are willing to give up some of your old destructive techniques, practices and behaviors. *Besides a healthy relationship, you are going to experience spiritual and personal growth, higher self-esteem and a much more satisfying life just by following the simple instructions in this manual.*

In the following pages we are going to address what works and what does not work, specifically in the relationship with your partner: wife, husband, boyfriend, girlfriend, or fiancé(e). You will also have some awareness exercises, which may give you insights into your own behavior and practices that you may not have been aware of and which do not serve you, or your relationship.

BEFORE YOU START

You may not even be in touch with your "ex", or your ex does not even talk to you. If this is your situation the first thing to do is to get back in communication with him/her so that you can use this Manual. The best way to do this is to apologize—in person (is the best), by phone, e-mail or mail—for whatever you did wrong. Leaving a letter casually where your partner can find it is a good way of doing it too. Do not make up reasons or excuses, and say that you promised to yourself and the world that you will never do it again. This is important: you have to actually MEAN it, believe it and keep your word about it, otherwise no one else will believe you. (Keep in mind that you may have promised things in the past and not kept your promise.) When I say apologize, I do not mean to merely say that you are "sorry." She/he already knows that. Most likely you said it before. What I do mean is use the word "apologize" instead of "sorry." Apologies do not cost *anything*. Also, do not apologize with an agenda of getting her/him back. This will become clearer as you read on. Do not do anything before you finish reading ALL of this Manual.

---

*   This manual is for mentally and emotionally healthy people and is in no way a substitute for professional medical treatment or counseling. I do not support your staying in an abusive relationship, whether you are an abuser or abused. In fact, *I do not encourage you to stay in any relationship whatsoever that you choose not to stay in.* Having a good relationship does not necessarily mean that you have to live, or even be, together.

A WORD ABOUT YOUR
FAMILY AND FRIENDS

Our family and friends often try to help us resolve the differences with our partners. How often do they succeed? Rarely. They most likely have not taken relationship classes either. In times of conflict with your partner (who is now quickly becoming your enemy), your family and friends "support you" by basically taking your side. That's what family does and that's what friends are for. The way they see it is as a friend's duty to "take your side" in an apparent "war" *against* your partner. That does not seem to be the best way to go about resolving your differences, does it? Those are most often the strategies for winning, or at least for not losing, a war. This manual is not about war; it's about peace. This manual is truly about DISSOLVING conflict and building a firm foundation for a healthy relationship.

Do not blame your family and friends for trying to help. You asked for it in the first place, remember? Love them, but do not follow their advice. In fact, do not even complain to them. They cannot remedy your situation. Only you can. If you are looking for sound advice, they cannot give it because they are too close to you. They may mean well, but they simply don't know; they learned from their parents and their parents learned from their parents, etc., who also didn't know. It goes down through generations. If you are honest with yourself you will see that by complaining you are just looking to your friends to support your *point of view*. It is very human to complain to your friends, but unfortunately not very effective. If you want your friends to support you, ask them to support your actions from this manual even if they do not agree or understand how it works.

Awareness Exercise: *Notice when you talk about your partner to others: What is it that you are saying? Are you complaining about him? What are you justifying? Are you looking for agreement? How would you react if your family and friends did not agree with your point of view? Notice that the more you talk about your partner's shortcomings, the more real they become, especially if you get the agreement. Consider that by complaining you are digging a deeper and deeper grave for your relationship.*

WORK

So, let's do some work now. Since you bought this manual, I presume that you have been doing everything in your power to save your relationship and you have not exactly succeeded. *I'm sure that you did your best.*

Now, you may not know what to do next or, you *know* that you've tried everything and there is nothing else you can do. Don't jump to conclusions just yet. Let's first see what you've been doing. What strategies and behaviors have you tried so far? Here are some examples. See which ones you can recognize as *yours* (not your partner's).

explaining	being in therapy and/or counseling ?
reasoning	praying
pressuring	hoping
being depressed	expecting him/her to change
more "loving"	expecting something
promising change	being in bad mood and/or depressed
threatening	moralizing
begging	throwing fits and tantrums
whining	pushing
bribing	being angry
arguing	having expectations
blaming	being a victim
justifying	complaining
asking	swearing
pleading	judging
avoiding	making him/her wrong
reassuring	being disrespectful
dominating	condescending
avoiding being dominated	seeking help from friends, etc.

I am sure you can find your actions among these and feel free to add your very own.

Awareness Exercise: *Underline the ones that sound familiar, then think for a moment and try to remember what outcomes you have achieved so far with the strategies and behaviors you have been using. Write them down if you wish.*

If you concluded that everything you have tried so far has not really worked, that there has been no major shift in the quality of your relationship, and now you don't know what you could possibly do more or differently, do not despair, there is light at the end of the tunnel.

After you've tried the above, you might have noticed that it does not work because **you cannot control the behavior of your partner**. *No matter what you think, you cannot have control over another person.* You never have and you never will. Only by changing your own behavior (remember the one that so far has not worked) will cause him to change in the way you want him to, in the way that you can love him and that he can love you. In fact, he is not going to "change", he will only start exhibiting his "good" side: the one that has always been there, the one that you loved in the first place. So, like with any other teamwork, in this relationship recovery program you will focus on *what YOU can do and who YOU can be in and for this relationship.*

The first thing to realize is that a *relationship is* for the most part *a game.* Now, you may be resistant to the notion of playing any games whatsoever. The relationship for you should not be a game at all, but a natural outcome of the affection for each other, or a similar notion. Nevertheless, you have been playing a game all along even if you thought that you hadn't. You've only played it by the "rules" that you "invented." This is by no means a casual game, but a game nevertheless.

The rules of the game in this manual guarantee that THERE ARE NO LOSERS. WHEN YOU WIN, EVERYONE WINS. The only way you can lose is if you stop playing by the rules of this manual, i.e., if you start playing a different game, the game that you've always played—and lost.

RULES

So here are the four rules of a *winning game*:

1. **STOP DOING WHATEVER IT IS YOU'VE BEEN DOING SO FAR THAT DID NOT WORK.**
   (Check the above list.)

> *"The definition of insanity*
> *is doing the same thing over and over again,*
> *expecting different results."*

> —*Rita Mae Brown*

Even by just NOT doing whatever you've been doing before and not doing anything instead, you will produce positive results. Easier said than done, you say. Well, it takes some thinking and practice to become *aware* of our actions, to catch ourselves in the act, to break the habit of being and living 'on automatic.'

Awareness Exercise: Just notice when you have the urge to react, when your buttons are pushed and then when you find the reasons and justifications to react in one of the ways mentioned above. You may even react and not be able to stop yourself at first. It is very important though, that you become aware of your knee-jerk reactions to her actions, her words, or even to your own thoughts. **Read this two more times.** *Read it again after every conversation with her that sounded confrontational and left you with a somewhat "bitter taste in your mouth."*

In order to take step number two, you always want to be aware of the following two concepts; they will help you be real and authentic and deal with confronting situations with more power, grace and self-confidence:

A. You Do Not *Need* Your Partner

As we said before, a relationship is a game. Professional athletes take games seriously but with a relaxed attitude. Any sports coach will tell you that you cannot be at your best if you are uptight and think only about how you must win. The trick is to *pay attention to your own performance* and strive for your own best.

Similarly with the relationship game, as long as you think that you cannot live without your partner, or in other words, that you must win her over, or that you really need her, or that you will "lose her" when she leaves, you cannot be relaxed enough to be able to win the game.

Whatever you may say, I assure you that you do not NEED her. You are just fine the way you are although you may not feel that way now. You were born alone and you will die alone and in the meantime you have a population of at least a few thousand people around you that you can have a relationship with.

Now, I understand that you WANT to be with your partner and that you WISH your partner were in love with you. So, having your partner in your life is more of a want or a wish than what you really need. Do you see the difference? Once you are able to recognize and accept this fact, you will breathe easier, you will see the reality easier, you will not be so much in your head thinking about what should or should not be, and you will not be driving yourself crazy. So, the choice is yours: if you are going to insist that you need her, you will suffer. If you let go of your neediness, you will gain power.

*Awareness Exercise: In the course of everyday life ask yourself a question whenever you see or hear or think of something you think you need: "Do I **really** need it, or I would merely like to have it or want it?" Notice when you start inventing 'reasons' for really needing something. There are actually VERY few things that you need and they are often connected to your very survival. Notice the difference between a want and a need.*

B. You Cannot Change The Past

> "In disagreements with loved ones,
> deal only with the current situation.
> Don't bring up the past."
>
> —*Dalai Lama*

Leave the past where it belongs: in the past. STOP fixing the past, because you cannot. Once it happens it's gone, you cannot bring it back, no one can change it unless you have a time machine. Do not dwell in past. What was done is done. You cannot do anything about it NOW. There is a sane alternative to changing the past: if you do not like it, invent another interpretation about what happened and/or start designing the future.

Someone said that if you really want tomorrow to be different than yesterday, you have to do something different TODAY.

Awareness Exercise: *Try to interpret past incidents in a way that allows you to deal with them easier. There are many interpretations to an occurrence. Just ask the other person you disagreed with and your friends. Everyone will give you a different interpretation. Take the one that is the most liberating for you. After all, there is truth in each and every one of them. Next, think instead about what you would like your relationship to be like; the relationship that will be satisfying for you. Create the future NOW.*

You've already started. This manual IS about creating a new future.

The next step is to replace everything you were doing that did not work with doing exactly the opposite of what you have been doing so far that did not work.

2. REVERSE THE PROCESS

Instead of disagreeing, agree. Instead of talking, listen. Instead of telling her about her, start talking about yourself. Acknowledging her possible assertion that for her this relationship does not work would be a good start. By acknowledging or agreeing to *whatever* she says—including her opinions about you and your relationship, you validate *her*. Her opinion may be right or wrong; it makes no difference. Your agreement is about your acknowledging her opinion—and she has every right to have an opinion and feel a certain way whether her thinking is right or wrong; it shows that you listen and acknowledge and validate her as a person. Whenever she says something, do not judge or assess. Just agree and shut up. There is a lot of "letting go" to do while practicing this second stage. The French say: "What you resist persists". Letting go of having to be right resolves the situation faster and is much less painful. You cannot change what has been said—it's in the past. Now there is an opportunity to create a new future just by acknowledging how she feels and letting go.

As you might see, agreeing with her about whatever she does or says does not mean that you are a weak, subservient human being controlled by her. On the contrary, by agreeing with her you will show your compassion and your understanding of where she comes from. In other words, you will exercise a power of listening: just noticing, accepting and acknowledging the way she thinks. She cannot but appreciate it. *Be sincere and authentic.* Ask genuine questions so that you can understand her better when appropriate, without pushing her buttons. Remember: do not bring up the past.

Often you will have the urge to explain how things are, or should be. Stop and just listen to HER explanations. If you normally were to reason with her, listen to her reasons for a change, acknowledge them and do not offer your counter arguments. If you used to pressure her into something, ask her what it is that she would like to do and just go along. Stop telling her that you love her. In fact, make her jealous. Have fun and go out by yourself. Show her that you can have a life outside of her. Show that you do not *need* her. If you were promising change, acknowledge that in the present situation it is very likely that nothing will change considering that nothing has worked so far and ask her what she wants to do about it. And so on. I hope you get the idea.

To follow this manual you will need some courage. Not needing her helps. Gaining power along the way by knowing the distinctions between reality and imagination, or facts and interpretations, also helps. Trusting the manual is essential. Do not regress to your old strategies, because . . . you are right: they do not work.

As you may notice, you are playing a game. You may also recognize that you do not like playing games.

That is exactly where we are heading—the no-game-zone, but for the time being, *the fact is—as we said before—that you have already been playing games all along but with a strategy that did not work.* What we have to do first is, *bring the relationship to the level of mutual support and respect by changing the rules of the game* where the two of you will be proud of each other. Then, when your relationship is repaired you can start building on it, go to the next level and make it a phenomenal relationship. But, for the time being, we must continue to play the game.

Another necessary ingredient in the strategy of this game is *your mood.*

3. HIGH SPIRITS, CHEERFULNESS AND HAPPINESS
are ABSOLUTELY necessary ingredients in this game.

Whenever you do something for him, do it gladly, immediately and exactly the way he wants it. The moment you decide to do something for him that you normally would not do, make up your mind, be sure that it is absolutely your choice to do this, that you do not expect anything in return, not even a 'thank you,' and that you will do it the best you can, not just merely do it. Remember that you've stopped being grouchy, controlling, complaining, etc., and that you are now adopting a strategy of doing things quite the opposite of what they were, i.e., instead of saying: "Here is your damn coffee," and throwing the cup on the table, you say: "How much sugar would you like?" while whistling your favorite song. Get the picture? Whatever is worth doing at all is worth doing well.

If you are not in a conversation, be cheerful. Show that you are happy with your life *at this moment;* that your happiness does not depend on his actions or inactions. YOU DO NOT NEED HIM. Show it by being happy. He likes you to be happy. He likes a "happy you," not a "grouchy you." It draws him closer. You did not get together in the first place because you logically assessed the situation as well as each other and only then logically decided to fall in love. Did you? You were 'happy together.'

No one wants to fight unless provoked, threatened and/or afraid. Avoid being threatening in any way and refrain from being provoked and feeling threatened. Always remember that you do not need him. Being happy is just as easily done as said. Try it and practice it. It is your choice from moment to moment. Happiness is a matter of now, of the present moment. You cannot be happy in the future or in the past.

Awareness Exercise: What do you achieve by being unhappy and grouchy? You get something out of it, some kind of satisfaction. What is it? Look deep and hard. What are the results in the quality of YOUR life when you are unhappy and grouchy? Compare what you are getting vs. what you are sacrificing. Read this two more times.

4. DO NOT TALK ABOUT YOUR RELATIONSHIP WITH YOUR PARTNER

Talk about movies, cooking, golf, or whatever. *Stop "working on your relationship and talking about it."* That strategy did not work either. Drop it. Remember this is a game. You do not talk about your relationship; you are on the court playing inside your relationship. (Remember when your relationship was at its best, say, not long after you'd met. Did you work on it to become that way?) You are already relating to him. All you do now differently is that you changed the rules. The game goes on.

Your changed behavior will result in his reconsidering staying in the relationship and wanting to have a good one too. And why wouldn't he? If he starts a new one, it is bound to end the same way as this one was before you changed the rules.

Once you give up fighting (disagreeing or resenting), he will too. He did not "win". You both won. A good relationship is a win/win game. As long as you keep insisting on being right—therefore he has to be wrong, or justifying your actions and invalidate his; as long as you are trying to play a one-upmanship game with him, the relationship will go down the tubes.

The price that you are paying for sticking to your old strategies has cost you a fulfilling relationship with him. When you give that up and stick with this manual, your relationship will start flourishing. Someone said that love was not gazing into each other's eyes, but looking into the future together. That is the next step in creating a powerful and satisfying relationship.

BE CAREFUL: *DO NOT SLIP INTO YOUR OLD BEHAVIOR* even if he does. Now you know what to do. The more you take responsibility for your relationship, the healthier it will be. (Responsibility is not a burden. It is a privilege. It is a STAND that you take FOR something.)

Awareness Exercise: What would happen if you were to take 100% responsibility for your relationship? Would that make you stronger, or weaker?

One day you may laugh at how silly, childish, immature, serious and significant you once were. Now you know better:

> Humans are not logical creatures when it comes to relationships.
> The relationship is a game.
> You cannot change the past.
> Do what works drop what doesn't.
> You do not NEED each other.

You cannot control the behavior of your partner.

You DO NOT have to be right.

You CAN be happy at any time.

You do not have to work ON the relationship—you are IN the relationship.

Do not complain to anyone who cannot do anything about it, like your friends and family.

You CAN choose what quality of relationship you want to have.

This is it for now. Apply what you've read here and your relationship will get repaired and both of you will become different people.

Going off with another partner is often the opportunity to make the same mistake again. First, repair the current relationship or marriage and then, if you want to find another partner, at least you will know how to keep her. The percentage of second marriage divorces is much higher than first ones. Does that tell you something?

FURTHER HELP

Once you repair your relationship you will start to build the next stage, a 'gameless' relationship. This will be the next level of your development too.

To ask further questions, or to share experiences and/or success stories please write to:

info@RelationshipSaver.com

For further coaching, support and guidance by phone or in person, through the process of recovering your relationship, or creating a better one I offer personal relationship counseling.

http://www.relationshipsaver.com/coaching.html

PART TWO

The Gameless Relationship

A practical guide to the
4 principles of a perfect relationship

I. INTRODUCTION

Why do you need to be in a *Gameless Relationship*?

In fact, you don't 'need' to be in a relationship at all, let alone a *Gameless Relationship*, but I invite you to consider what a *Gameless Relationship* has to offer.

A *Gameless Relationship* is a relationship where we appreciate and accept each other and ourselves for what and who we are, no more and no less. In a *Gameless Relationship* we relate to each other and ourselves with love, respect and compassion. There are no games played.

We do not manipulate, dominate, coerce, strategize, survive, control, defend, prevail, resist, or force an outcome. We do not blame others or ourselves, justify our actions, give reasons or make excuses. Most importantly, we do not lie, cheat or deceive.

It is an environment where you are free to grow, develop, prosper and be content and happy. It is the context for constantly creating and recreating yourself, your relationship and your life. In the long run, it is the only relationship worth having. It is the kind of relationship that will allow you to blossom into your full potential.

Being in a *Gameless Relationship* takes care of several crucial issues in our lives:

— Security
— Self-knowledge
— Self-esteem and self-respect
— Freedom to be true to yourself
— Practical knowledge of dealing with many adverse life situations
— Being clear about many areas of "whys" and "hows" of everyday life challenges.

Being in a *Gameless Relationship* often requires courage to experience adventure and abundance.

The skills and rigor required for being in a *Gameless Relationship* will allow you to have more love and freedom in your life as well as in your relationship. It will also bring you respect and credibility from the people around you.

Children growing up in such a relationship become psychologically healthy, happy and successful human beings. You will also notice that being in a *Gameless Relationship* with your *significant other* carries over into your other relationships resulting in less stress and disappointment.

In this book we will cover four basic principles, guidelines and skills that always need to be present in your life in order to have such a relationship. Using these skills on a daily basis will help you *achieve personal happiness, joy and success beyond what you may believe is possible right now!*

Awareness Exercise: *Consider your present, or past relationship (if you are not in one now), and notice what is/was missing. Make a list of all the things that could be increased, decreased, better or different. I suggest that you put it in writing rather than just doing a mental exercise. Keep the list for future reference.*

II. WHAT IS IN YOUR WAY?
WHAT IS STOPPING YOU?

The answer to these questions may come as a surprise to you. At first, you may strongly disagree, but I think deep inside you know the answer. Even if the answer to these questions is not 100% correct, I again suggest that for the time being you consider it as an absolute and irrevocable truth.

The reason I am asking you to consider that EVERYTHING you read in the following pages is true is not because I say so. I ask you to accept it as the truth because *it works*. In other words, I am inviting you to put it into practice with a leap of faith that all that you read in the following pages is the truth. Then, assess the results only after some reasonable period of time after implementing these principles to see if they produce results for you.

Please also keep in mind that having knowledge of the principles that you will read in the following pages will make no difference in your life and your relationship unless you put them into practice immediately. You may fail miserably at the beginning, and you may even do things that you do not "feel like doing." However, as you get better and more consistent in their application, your life will correspondingly transform not merely for the better. It may even take a *quantum leap* beyond what you might have ever thought possible.

Now back to the barriers to your having a *Gameless Relationship*. All sorts of reasons come to mind when we think about why we do not have what we want or why things are not working out for us.

In other words, when something does not work, we first look for the reason outside of ourselves. There are circumstances, conditions, situations, the environment and/or the "other person" or others. When we eventually find the reason (and we always can) we realize that quite often we have no power to do anything about it. At such times we get angry and disappointed and fear often sets in. We feel powerless. We give up and lose hope.

However, we very rarely consider the possibility that somehow WE may be the cause of whatever is in the way of succeeding in our lives and relationships. Even if we do come to the conclusion that we may be the cause, it is usually in the context of making ourselves wrong, thinking it is our fault or our mistake. We blame ourselves. We very rarely, if ever, think that we actually have the power to deal with ANY situation in which we find ourselves. This is especially true when it comes to our own thoughts and emotions. We are rarely aware that we actually have the choice when it comes to our uniquely human capacity to make interpretations of, and give meanings to our experiences and the events in our lives.

Healthy, adult human beings are equipped and able to fully and consciously experience any emotion without automatically reacting, acting it out or being overwhelmed by it. We will see in the following chapters how you can completely be in control of your life.

So, at the very beginning I invite you to consider that what stands in the way of your having a *Gameless Relationship* and having a fulfilling life is YOU. The buck stops with you. ALWAYS. The environment always reacts to us and we do not have to always react to the environment. We will see that we always have a choice on a conscious level as opposed to instinctive or automatic reactions.

Awareness Exercise: Notice your resistance to my invitation to "consider [all that you read here] as an absolute and irrevocable truth." Also, notice how sometimes you have particular thoughts and beliefs that stop you from taking actions that you know for certain would be good for you. Or, ponder how you sometimes do something that you know does not serve you, but you "cannot help it" and do it anyway. How much does "resisting" stop you from being who you want to be? How often do you think that that's just "who you are" and give into the resistance?

III. GENDER DIFFERENCES

In order to begin to better understand our own nature and the nature of our relationships, let us now examine the design of the two sexes. Human beings are divided in two basic types, male and female. We are all very aware of some obvious constant patterns of *sameness* or *differences* between the sexes. However, men and women are not only different—they are literally opposite. That's why we say, *the opposite sex*. Here we will concentrate on *a no-choice option*, the differences that are inherent and instinctual in us and that we most of the time cannot and often would not do anything about. Just to understand them and distinguish them as such will make a big difference in your relationships.

As human beings, men and women are two different types by natural and genetic design. Our different biologically pre-determined roles, and therefore needs, are still deeply ingrained in us because they have been necessary for our own survival and the survival of our offspring for thousands of years. If we did not develop certain habits and roles when having to rely on each other for thousands of years in a very hostile and dangerous environment, humans would have become extinct a long time ago. Along the way these habits and behaviors particular to each gender have proven to work rather well.

There are more then 6,000,000,000 of us walking the earth today, twice as many as when I was in school. These different behaviors and ways of being have been permanently programmed into our genes. In other words, they have become instinctual behaviors, which by necessity have developed to be very different for women then for men. Later we'll see what they are and learn to recognize and appreciate them. The knowledge and ability to recognize these behaviors and not take them personally could lead to a much more harmonious relationship, or a *Gameless Relationship*.

Our instinctual, genetically predetermined self is just one facet of who we are. We are also spiritual, thinking and reasoning beings able to distinguish between the past and the future due to the further development of our brain, the frontal lobe. This is what makes us different from all the other species and in that way we are unique on this planet. Although these characteristics do not serve us well all the time, it has allowed us to be who we are today, at the top of the food chain.

By using our reasoning and thinking powers we have the opportunity to question and reverse our instinctual, subconscious, knee-jerk reactions to everyday events.

We have the opportunity to consciously choose.

As we said earlier, although we can choose how to react to whatever we face in life, most of the time our reactions are instinctive. Our buttons get pushed; we react as we have in the past in similar situations. We do all this without giving it a second thought.

Problems often arise when we assume that men and women go through a similar process of thinking in a particular situation. Men often lament as to why women are so complicated and why they cannot be simpler, *like us*. Women on the other hand see men as hairy women and cannot conceive that anyone can possibly be so simple. They often want to change their men into a *perfect woman*. Another distinct characteristic of men is that men more often than not say exactly what they mean; women rarely do. When a man makes a statement, women immediately start thinking what that might mean. She often thinks, especially in times of relationship crises, that there must be a hidden meaning behind his words. She cannot conceive that he can possibly be so simple as to say exactly what he means, no more, no less.

These are just a couple of examples where it becomes apparent that we ARE different and in most cases we cannot help it. And, there is a reason for our differences that we will shortly discover. The most we can do in many situations is to recognize the difference and act appropriately. That being said, let's see what are some of the basic differences between men and women, and why we are so different. We will also address the issue as to how to deal with these differences, so that we can contribute to each other. By the way, this is by no means a complete study of male/female differences, but I would like to mention some basic ones as an illustration of how men and women are inherently different, in addition to their physical appearance.

Men Are Hunters

Men are *bigger* and *stronger*. They put food on the table; they are *providers*. They want to *impress* women with bigger and better "deer", or money, car, position, intelligence, physical strength and more. They also do all this because they want to make their women happy. A hunter carries a spear and is always focused on the deer (read: task at hand). He always wants to know *what the point is*, to see a general picture without much detail. He can always come back to details later. He has no patience or time to listen to woman's stories, which seem to have no point.

He first needs to know what the point of a conversation is in order decide whether to engage in it further.

The hunter's duty is to solve problems and find solutions and produce results (read: catch a deer). That's why men get immersed in their work and careers. Additionally, men are single focused and they sometimes seem to disconnect in a conversation. For example, a man cannot be *busy* and pay attention to his woman at the same time; otherwise the *deer* will escape.

Men are direct. They talk straight. They mean what they say. No more and no less. (Coordinating a hunt leaves no room for stories or messages with hidden meanings or ulterior motives). Men need to feel confident and in control. Otherwise, they will not be able to catch that proverbial deer and put food on the table.

What can women do to avoid frustration and hurt that may result from a hunter's behavior which can easily be interpreted as *"he does not care"* or *"if he loved me he would not do that"*, or . . . (fill in you own favorite)?

To start with, do not take what he says personally, and start finding ways to appreciate those qualities in men because they are useful.

Secondly, stop expecting your man to behave and think like you, or like some image that you have of a perfect woman. He is not just a *Hairy Woman*. He is a different species. He is and will always be a man. Instead, try to provide an environment of encouragement so that he can be a *man*, feel in charge, in control and confident.

Women need to stop "castrating men," as Alison Armstrong, the creator of *"Celebrating Men, Satisfying Women"*, has said. What she means by that, among other things, is putting your man down and showing him disrespect in front of others.

Try also to accept that when men commit to women they do so only when they are ready. Nagging will not make men commit to anything. Men do things for their women because they love to see them happy and satisfied.

Readiness for men is an "inside job"; it has nothing to do with a woman. Only when he is ready from inside himself can he own his choice. This cannot be forced or manipulated.

Also, when men decide to do things for their women they do them because they love to see them happy and satisfied. Help them decide to take care of you. Tell them what you need and how you need it. Do not demand it. In fact, one of the generally forgotten roles of women is to tell their men not only what they want more of, but also, when it is enough. If they do not, men will keep "hunting" and bringing home deer after deer, not knowing when to stop. In today's societies women seem to encourage men to bring home more and more of whatever it is they bring out of general fear of "not having enough" to somehow survive. Man, on the other hand, will keep bringing more and more of whatever makes his woman happy (money, jewelry, houses, power, social prestige, machismo, protection). It's no wonder we are ruining our environment and cutting our lifeline out from underneath us.

Our societies are depleting natural resources. Women can take some responsibility for it and be very effective at slowing the process of destruction by men if they would only tell men when to stop and not encourage them to keep "hunting."

In addition to hunting, a man's duty is to protect his woman. Men *love* protecting their women. What would be useful for a woman to understand is that if a man is angry with her, or complains about her, it does not mean that he is ready to abandon her. A woman would do that, but a man never would. In order to lessen a man's dominance in such situations, a woman would often withdraw and lash out at a man with the intention to lessen the man's power and dissipate the potential threat. This is again what Alison Armstrong calls *"emasculating or castrating men."* This kind of behavior is not supportive of a *Gameless Relationship* and being aware of this instinctual reaction would make a big difference in your relationship.

Women Are Gatherers

Women are pleasers. And for a good reason: they are smaller and much weaker then men. Fear for their physical safety is always present, whether they are by themselves or in the presence of other men who are either loud or angry. In order to practice their skills as gatherers, and to have time to raise a family, they are dependent on stronger and bigger men to bring home food and to protect them. Women are always concerned about how their men feel and always strive to please them. Being weaker and smaller, women are constantly worried about their physical safety and their survival. No wonder women depend on men. That is how it was for a cave woman and that's how it is now for women most of the time. This again is an instinctual reaction that is always present and much stronger no matter if a woman's rational mind tells her differently. Men are mostly completely unaware of their overwhelming strength and women's deep-seated fears resulting from this enormous difference.

Women, being the gatherers, also bring food to the table. They provide, but do not see themselves as providers. In fact, most women resent being providers. When gatherers gather food, they do so by having a diffused awareness and keen attention to detail (necessary to find berries which are not poisonous). Gatherers have to be closely connected to nature as well as to other people. They learn by exchanging detailed information. That's why women generally seem to talk much more.

Gatherers need to be closely connected in order to exchange information. They cannot afford to "check out" by being single focused. They are also very intuitive. For instance, they do not understand how men can be so "insensitive" as to "not know" what they want, even without their verbalizing it. Women often expect their men to be as intuitive and emotionally connected to women as women are to each other. They expect men to have the ability to "read their minds." As we said, men are single focused and cannot afford to read minds. It's too unpredictable. They need concrete data otherwise the deer will escape. So, men *need to be told* by women in no uncertain terms what it is that a woman wants. Men CANNOT read minds.

Women's natural drive is to sustain life. They are nurturers and builders. They would never "kill for an idea," as opposed to men who are too often ready to do just that. Women know what's "good and bad" for you. They are also healers.

What can men do to avoid being frustrated by perceived endless chattering, detailed instructions and demands? First, do not expect women to be like men. In other words, communicate and relate to them. Share your feelings and do not give laconic answers. The less you share the details of your life and your feelings the more she thinks that you do not love her, or that there is something wrong and that you may abandon her. That is because the more details a woman tells about what happened to her in a given situation the more she trusts you. When a woman talks to a man a lot it is a good sign for a man. Men do not have to remember all the details that have "no point". Just understand that a talkative woman is a trusting woman. When women get silent, it's time to worry.

Women take things personally. Always keep that in mind. If you ask her if anything is wrong, never take the first explanation for granted or as a true answer. If you feel that something is wrong even though she denies it, keep asking. She wants to please you and would not necessarily tell you the truth right away. The real story may come out after the fifth try, and only if you change your attitude so that she feels safe. If you want the truth you need to work for it.

Men identify with their opinions and are very protective of them. On the other hand, women invest much less in their opinions. It is much easier for women to change their minds, even to accept your opinion. That does not mean that they are "spineless" and that they can be manipulated.

No matter what men think, by nature's design, women are usually in charge. They pick their men and not vice versa. Just think of who's courting whom. Men would do well to listen to women more often. If nothing else, we would have much more peace, love and nurturing instead of warring, cutthroat and competitive societies. If it were not for women, men would have probably exterminated our species by now.

Men should take the time to remind and explain to their women that they cannot read minds. Women need to ask for what they want and sometimes have to instruct men in detail. For example, "My birthday is next week and I want flowers." Let your woman know that if you do not do things of your own accord it does not mean that you do not love her.

Note: Most of the Gender Differences section was adapted from Alison Armstrong's material. Thank you, Alison. *http://www.understandmen.com/*

Awareness Exercise: *Pay attention to your expectations for your partner to think, reason, do things or come to the same and "obvious" conclusions that you would. Do not assume that your partner and you are the same. She/he is a different type of human being and his or her brain is not wired the same way as yours. See if you can get interested and even fascinated by the way your significant other functions and accept it instead of hoping for it to change. Let go of constantly expecting the impossible and blaming the other person when you don't get it.*

IV. FOUR BASIC PRINCIPLES OF A
Gameless Relationship

Without integrity, responsibility, commitment and love, we drift through life constantly having similar problems over and over again. Having a satisfying life and a *Gameless Relationship* is impossible without these, so let's describe them in some detail.

1. INTEGRITY

Nothing works without it.

Integrity means being whole and complete at every moment without anything missing. Integrity also means workability. If an airplane has an engine missing it cannot fly. If it cannot fly, if it does not work, it is partly disintegrated. The same thing applies to people. Our engine is our language, our word, our conversations, promises and declarations. Integrity is all about promises and declarations.

The following formula is a very simple and yet very powerful one for making effective promises.

Promise: I will do X by, or at time Y.

When you make a promise you must be very clear what it is that you are promising. The first part in the formula, X, cannot be vague, like "I promise to make you happy". It must be something specific and measurable, something that will be very clear to all concerned parties whether it was fulfilled or not. For instance, when you promise to meet someone at a particular place the address may not be enough. You must also include other details like store name, apartment number, which floor, directions and landmarks.

The second part, Y, has to be bound in time otherwise it isn't a promise. It becomes just empty talk, an interesting story. Empty promises are usually ones without a time line. It is very deceiving and if done on purpose very manipulative.

When we break a promise we are out of integrity. If we keep breaking promises we lose integrity altogether—we disintegrate, we lose our credibility, and our words become meaningless. We become ineffective in the world and every accomplishment is very hard if not impossible to achieve. The surest and shortest way to failure is to not keep your promises.

A high level of integrity is essential for a successful relationship. Just imagine a relationship without integrity, where promises are not fulfilled and where lying, cheating, and deceiving are the order of the day. Do you think that this way of being can lead to a successful relationship, let alone a *Gameless* one?

A promise may also come in the form of a simple "yes" or "I do." A promise does not have to be explicitly voiced. It may be implied such as when you get your driver's license. The implied promise is that you will obey traffic rules. It also may be something that others expect of you, something that you do routinely, or that is customary or implicitly your responsibility, like taking care of your children.

Sometimes, in spite of our best intentions we cannot keep our promises. In order to regain our credibility when that happens, we can do two things; either renegotiate the promise, or apologize and re-promise. Either way, we must first recognize and acknowledge that we are not going to keep the original promise, or that we have broken it. This can be a difficult task, one we often want to avoid by finding reasons and excuses for not keeping our word. Naturally, we always want to look good. However, this often leads to the further "disintegration" of our integrity.

Personal Integrity

Keeping your word

True respect cannot be demanded; it can only be freely given.

Personal integrity starts with honoring your word as yourself. Words can either "make us, or break us" in everyday life. The words that directly relate to the use or misuse of this power are promises and declarations. Standing behind what you say is what earns you respect, trust, and ultimately happiness and fulfillment. You are as good as your word and so is your life.

"Honoring your word as yourself" does not mean that you have to keep your word every time you make a promise and it certainly does not mean that you should beat yourself up when you don't. What it means is that you always honor your word to the extent that you honor yourself. People with low self-esteem will always find a reason or excuse for *not* keeping their word. They will always blame and find fault with others, circumstances, or themselves.

Taking responsibility for being in integrity becomes a difficult task if you have no respect for yourself. The more you respect yourself the more you will make sure you keep your word and vice versa. In time it becomes a self-fulfilling prophecy. Broken promises lead to distrust in your abilities to produce results and loss of self-respect and respect from others. On the other hand, the less often you break your promises the more you will respect, honor and like yourself. It is either an upward or downward spiral. If you respect yourself others will respect you too.

How do you keep your word?

The first step is to always put your promises "into existence." One way is to write them down. In order to ensure that your promises will be fulfilled and that you will not forget, make it a habit to write them down in your calendar. It is also a good idea to write down the promises that others make to you. Writing them down gives them existence in the "real" world and they are less likely to be "forgotten." There is no such thing as "I forgot." What happened is that you didn't put it into existence in some form or fashion so that you can be reminded about it. Not putting your promises into existence may be a conscious or subconscious intention not to keep it.

The second step is to create support for your intention to keep your word. Support could include reminders like alarms, signals, notes and asking other people to remind you of your promise. Different kinds of reminders are appropriate for different people and for different kinds of promises. Make your own system that works for you. Also, surround yourself with friends and people who will support and help you keep your word, instead of buying into your sometimes very convincing, elaborate and believable stories and excuses. This does not mean that they have to beat you up about it, but just to remind you of your lack of authenticity about it.

How do you not keep your word and still be in integrity? How do you revoke your word responsibly?

You might think that it is nearly impossible to always keep your word. I agree. But, there are some rules that you should keep in mind about not keeping your promises. The rules are simple: the more notice you give from the date of the deadline, or the sooner you revoke your promise the more you maintain your integrity and credibility. By withdrawing your promise the moment you realize that you may not be able to keep it, you show respect and consideration for the other person. If it's not too late, you can always renegotiate and/or re-promise. Either way, accept responsibility and accept the consequences.

If you do not keep your word and the deadline has passed—as surely will happen sometimes—the only thing you can do is apologize, promise that it will not happen again and re-promise, if appropriate.

Do not give reasons for not keeping your word unless asked to do so. You can always make up really good reasons for not keeping your promises. Your reasons may be very real and true, but no matter how reasonable they are if you keep breaking your word you WILL lose credibility. What is often required is being UN-reasonable about keeping your promises. When you break your promise an apology and a promise not to do it again is sufficient. If your apology is not accepted, you must accept the consequences. On the other hand, as stated before, revoking your promises and/or frequently not keeping your word will erode your credibility. You will not be seen as trustworthy and you will have to work very hard at being heard and believed again.

This may become very frustrating, as you will tend to blame others for not trusting you and believing what you are trying to communicate. If you lie once to your partner and you are caught, you will have to keep proving yourself over and over for a very long time. Ruining your credibility and trust does not take much effort. Keeping it intact, on the other hand, requires energy, diligence and rigor. Following the path of least resistance is a sure road to failure. Always take responsibility for failing to keep your word, promise not to do it again and this time keep your word, no matter what. In the end, you may or may not be forgiven.

What is the most common and universal reason for not keeping our word?

Whenever we promise something we have a reason for promising it, otherwise why would we promise anything? At the same time, the reason for promising something is most often the same reason for breaking our promises. You may think this makes no sense, but consider that when the reason for promising something changes or disappears, you are likely to break your promise because the reason for promising is not there anymore.

So, why bother keeping the promise, you may ask? If the name of the integrity game is to keep your promise, then the *only* way to do so is to disregard the reason for making the promise in the first place, and keep your word *just because you gave it*. Honor your word, instead of honoring the reasons and circumstances. If you honor your reasons and when the reason for promising change, you may feel justified in breaking your word.

For example, you feel like going to a movie because you've heard it was good and you promised to meet your date in front of the cinema. In the meantime, you hear that the movie is really not as good as you were made to believe and of course now you do not feel like seeing the movie. Consequently, you break your word and do not show up at the cinema. Do you think you'll have a second date? Not a chance—not even with anyone remotely acquainted with your date!

The word about your credibility, or lack thereof, spreads fast and takes a long time to correct. If you don't want this to happen, you will show up at the cinema regardless. Be there just because you promised. Apply this to every area of your life, especially in your relationships and the quality of your life will start transforming. Do not consider some promises to be more important than others. Treat ALL promises as equally important. Once you give a promise it is not about what you promised any more, it's about YOU.

Declarations

Making and honoring your declarations is an even higher level of integrity. Giving your word, or promising is usually about DOING (or not doing) something. Declaration, on the other hand, is more about BEING as opposed to merely doing. It includes both. Who you are determines what you say, how you listen, and what you do. In fact, you may declare yourself to be whoever you want to be.

Declaration is a very powerful act of creation. Declaration is not determined by your past. Declaration is an act of creation of the future you choose to step into. I am sure you have already declared yourself, or accepted another's declaration about who you are in many different roles. For example, you are a father or mother, employee, boss, girlfriend or boyfriend, responsible for this or that, businessman, spiritual person, vegetarian, great lover, smart, cool, hot, good listener, compassionate friend and many more.

Living up to and being consistent with who you declare yourself to be is the ultimate way of being in integrity. If your actions in your everyday life are not consistent with your declaration about who you are, then you compromise your integrity and your honor. When you do this, your self-respect plummets and you lose credibility, Influence and respect with your family, friends, colleagues and community.

Declarations, as stated earlier, do not have to be formal. Sometimes they sound like promises and sometimes they blend into conversations. They should always be treated seriously because other people will remember what you say and they will notice if you are being inconsistent with what you have said or declared. If you are not consistent, again, your integrity, credibility and respect may suffer with these people. Remember the saying, *"Actions speak louder than words?"*

Purposeful declarations that are well thought out can be the most powerful tool for achieving great relationships, successful careers, reaching any goal that you set for yourself and creating the future of your choice. They are the declarations that do not merely match or describe you, but the ones that are bold enough and big enough to pull you and your relationships to a higher level. It is much more powerful to declare that you have a great relationship and make sure that you do, no matter how difficult, than to simply describe your relationship as you think it is now. In other words, move from the ordinary or mundane to a standard of excellence.

Never underestimate the power of declarations made by people known who have high levels of integrity. Recall the Declaration of Independence that gave birth to The United States of America, or President Kennedy's declaration about the U.S. being on the Moon in ten years. Both of these declarations were powerful because they moved things forward and neither of them seemed possible at the time they were made.

We generally perceive that we have two distinct types of problems. One set of problems is the one that arises because there is something to fix in order to "survive." The other set of problems is the one that we intentionally create by declaring something in existence and then solving the problems that we need to deal with in order to fulfill our declared dream. Since there is no life without problems, which of the two problems would you rather have?

Integrity of conversations with others

Conversation is the basic tool for relating. Conversations consist of speaking *and* listening and the latter seems to be far more important than the former. Contrary to popular belief, it is far more important how we choose to listen than what we choose to say. What we say is always a reaction to what we hear. What we hear depends on *what* we listen for and to *whom* we listen.

Very often, when we are in a conversation we do not hear what is being said, but what *we think* is being said. We spend more time having a conversation with ourselves about what is being said, i.e., judging, assessing, comparing to our experiences, thinking about what we will say next, and more. All of this instead of being genuinely interested in what the other person is really trying to communicate.

You really do have a choice in how you want to listen to the other person. Do you choose to listen to the other person as if "he/she has no idea about what he/she is talking about" or can you choose to listen for a "contribution to you?" This choice is entirely yours no matter what reasons you could possibly find to the contrary. In fact, you can alter the conversation and the whole relationship quite drastically, more by how you choose to listen than by the choice of your words. The way you listen to your partner is also a matter of integrity.

One of the ways to improve your relationship is to put integrity into every conversation. This also means that each and every conversation needs to be *whole and complete*. If it is not, results won't be produced. We all know the experience of an incomplete conversation. For whatever reason we cut the conversation short without making sure that we said whatever we needed to say or allowed our partners to fully express themselves making sure that we truly understood the message.

If conversations cannot be completed in a continuous period of time, then arrange to finish them at a set time in the future. The point is to not leave conversations unfinished because wrong conclusions will be drawn, misinterpretations will abound, and people will get upset. Erroneous meanings are created from incomplete conversations. These misguided conclusions become the basis for the next, often unrelated interactions, which widen the communication gap.

This is often how relationships get into trouble. Little problems become bigger and the snowball effect can destroy the relationship. It happens too often in conversations and other modes of communication. In particular, avoid using e-mails and instant messaging to communicate anything but urgent and simple information. There is simply too much room for misinterpretation using these communication methods.

Integrity Of Conversations With Ourselves

You know that little voice inside which is always present no matter what you do, whether you are alone or in conversation with someone? At this point you may wonder, what voice? Precisely, THAT voice. The one that is always judging and assessing, blaming other people, circumstances, and even you. Whenever you have conversations with yourself where you make yourself wrong, bad, or inferior in any way you are not contributing to being your 'whole and complete' self. Therefore, by definition, you are out of integrity. You are disintegrating.

Think about times when you are depressed, when you make yourself wrong, when you feel guilty. Don't you feel that you are somehow not whole and complete, that something is obviously missing? I don't care what moral, societal standards, or religions teach about all of this. The fact is that you are not fully operational, or at your best at these times and therefore you are OUT of integrity. Feeling guilt and self-pity, beating yourself up about anything that you've done in the past or worrying about the future is out of integrity.

The way to get back into integrity is to take action. What I mean by action is get into conversation. Clean things up. If you cannot, or do not want to do that, then simply give it up or release it. Feeling bad or working against your own best interests is not serving anyone, least of all you. In these situations there is an opinion, belief, position or attachment to give up. Can you do it? In fact, it is much simpler than you think. Give it a try and you'll see. All it takes is a declaration of giving it up. Make it public if possible, declaring it in someone else's presence.

Integrity of a relationship

A relationship is a unit, and the people in the relationship can jointly, as a unit, assume responsibilities that are in one way or another made known to the outside world. We, as a couple, a family or partners, must be consistent with who we have declared ourselves to be to the outside world, to our children, relatives, friends, and organizations. The fulfillment of promises given to other people individually and/or as a "we" becomes the full responsibility of *each one* of "us."

Keeping an EMPOWERING CONTEXT for all of your conversations is the bottom line of what integrity is all about. Any disempowering conversation that may lead to the disintegration of your relationship, or your own potential as a human being, leads to loss of integrity. This includes gossip, complaints to people who can do nothing about the particular issue, making others wrong, justifying your actions, trying to dominate others, lying, cheating and deceiving, manipulating, or forcing an outcome. I think you get the picture.

Let me summarize why integrity is so important for a healthy relationship:

— A relationship that is not in integrity, whole and complete and functional at every moment is not a stable relationship. In order to bring stability into it, you first need to bring it into integrity.

— The trust, security and stability of a relationship depend on individual integrity.

It is very difficult to rely on, build any kind of future, develop trust in, or be on a daily basis with someone who does not keep their word (spoken or implied). This is whether it's about the marriage vows, coming home on time for dinner or anything in between. Integrity has no gradations. It's like being pregnant. You cannot be more in integrity or less so, you either are or you are not in this or that particular case. You either keep your word or you don't.

— Therefore, be in integrity in your relationship and you will assure a *Gameless Relationship*.

— Ultimately, in a *Gameless Relationship* each person is 100% responsible for the integrity of the relationship. (See RESPONSIBILITY below.)

— NEVER compromise your integrity.

Awareness Exercise: *How often do you feel bad after you break your promise? Or, has it become a habit for you and you've got really good at finding good, true and real reasons for not keeping your word? What percent of the time would you say that you are in integrity? Does that work for you and your relationship?*

How often do you have conversations, whether you initiate them or not, where no one is any better off after it's finished? Who are you? Who have you declared yourself to be? How much in integrity is your relationship, 20%, 60% or 100%?

2. RESPONSIBILITY

Responsibility starts with the willingness to be the cause in the matter of your life.

Responsibility means, "Being able and willing to respond." In life we often *react automatically* to events, other people, or our own thoughts and feelings. When we react, we often do so automatically without conscious awareness, which can often turn out to be highly inappropriate and contrary to our best interests. (See The Relationship Saver.)

So, what is it that hinders our ability to respond appropriately? We are doing what we have always done in the past. We re-ACT, which means that our own interests or the interests of the relationship are not served. We act the same way we acted before to a similar situation. If we don't get the result we want, "we do *more of the same,* hoping that it will produce different results". By the way, this is the definition of insanity.

Responding appropriately, or being response-able, means taking everything into consideration (including our own thought process) and then making a free choice. When you make a choice in this way it becomes *your* choice, and you must own it. Such a choice cannot be made by someone who is a victim of circumstances; rather, it becomes an expression of your free will. Being responsible starts with your willingness to be accountable in the matter and deal with situations from the viewpoint that you are the generator of your choices. Your choices reflect who you are, what you do and what you have. Again, this is not the truth; it is an empowering stand that you can choose to take.

Since we truly can choose how we see a situation and how we interpret it, we have the power to be able to respond appropriately to whatever situation we find ourselves in. In other words, we always have an opportunity to empower ourselves by taking responsibility for whatever happens to us. This is an empowering choice that any one of us can take. The question is: Are you willing to be fully responsible for the quality of your life? Are you willing to give up thoughts, feelings and actions that do not serve you, or your relationship? Are you willing to reconsider and re-examine your interpretations of events and beliefs that reflect your judgments and declare yourself to be the master of your own destiny? Are you willing to be unreasonable enough to act in your best interest and the best interest of your relationship—no matter what? Or, will you settle for merely being a victim of your circumstances?

Responsibility is not a burden, nor is it fault, blame, credit, shame or guilt. It is a stand we take. It is a willingness to be the cause in the matters of our lives, to be fully accountable for our lives. In accepting responsibility, we put ourselves in the powerful position of being the creators of our lives. No one else can give it to us nor can we bestow the responsibility onto others, it is the power and the grace that only we can give to ourselves.

Now, consider what it would be like to be 100% responsible for your relationship in the way that we have defined responsibility. Since you cannot make your partner responsible—responsibility is a gift you can only give to yourself—the 50/50 concept of responsibility is doomed to failure. Have you noticed that if you take 50% responsibility for your relationship, whenever something goes wrong that it is up to the other person's 50% to fix it? In effect, you have no control over it.

Unless you accept 100% responsibility for whatever happens in your relationship, you are on a slippery slope to failure. You give away your power by giving away the responsibility (read: power of choice) for your relationship and your life to someone else.

The truth is that no one else really wants to be responsible for your life anyway. The other people involved usually see it as a burden. Not being responsible for your own life is a cop-out. All we get is the perverse pleasure of blaming others and justifying our position. It is the source of all complaints and the recipe for becoming a victim. It is a road to failure and a miserable life of victim-hood. Once you decide to embrace responsibility it will prove to be your doorway to freedom.

So, are you willing to have a *Gameless Relationship*? If you are, then consider taking 100% responsibility for your relationship and you will be on the road to achieving it.

Awareness Exercise: *How often do you find yourself complaining and blaming others? Notice when you are doing this, especially when something undesirable happens. Go back into the past and see where you could have done something different, to have avoided finding yourself in the present undesirable situation. (See The Relationship Saver.) Play a "what if" game with yourself. No one has to know. Beware of finding excuses, justifications and reasons. Be rigorous and find reasons* **to take responsibility***, instead of how to avoid it. Anyone can do this. You may be surprised how peaceful you will feel and empowered you will become.*

3. COMMITMENT

If you do not know what you are committed to, look at your life.

You've heard people who say they want to be in a "committed" relationship, and there are others who say that they want to avoid it. The latter somehow seems to apply more often to men than women. And that seems to be biologically natural.

Men have much less to lose and much more to gain by not committing to one woman for too long. This is how men are genetically programmed. The biological reality is that men have an infinite number of sperm during their lifetime because they keep producing them every day by the millions. Women on the other hand are born with a finite number of eggs. Women do not make more eggs during their lifetime, so they'd better be careful not to waste too many of them.

Also, when a child is born it is always clear who the mother is, but not necessarily so with the father. Therefore, the mother is the one who is "stuck" with the child and the one who has to take responsibility for the child's future, not to mention the initial nine months of pregnancy, pain from childbirth and the risk of death while giving birth. In other words, a woman puts her life on the line to have a relationship with a man. That's why, contrary to popular opinion, women rarely "date." They are either in a relationship or not. Not so with men. Men can afford to date. Women cannot.

As you can see, biologically speaking, a woman has a lot more to invest (and therefore more to lose) in a relationship then a man. A man can hop from woman to woman, making children without any investment or risk. Humans and other non-monogamous animals instinctively know this. This concept affects our thinking about morals, ethics, fidelity and sexual freedom, or the lack of it.

We said before that men are bigger and stronger. They do not *need* anyone to guard their physical safety. They can survive on their own much easier than women. Therefore, men sometimes perceive a commitment as an unnecessary burden and not as a life or death necessity. Not so with women. For a woman having a man in her life is often perceived as a life-or-death proposition.

The reason I mention this is not to excuse men for being promiscuous, nor justify women for being intentional and sometimes desperate about marriage. Generally speaking, cultures are built as an expression of our genetic programming. Marriage is a socially created institution in order to ensure that women are taken care of while they care for their offspring. The importance of virginity is so that men cannot deny their fatherhood. And, the importance of woman's fidelity is to protect a man from raising someone else's children. Man's fidelity, on the other hand, is important for a woman because if a man is not faithful a woman experiences fear of abandonment. For a woman, it could be, or feel like, a life or death issue.

All of the aforementioned is integrated into all of the religions and customs of societies and cultures around the world and is still observed and practiced despite the emancipation of women (by the birth control pill, freezing of eggs for later use, and other scientific advances). We have now come to an age when we want successful and happy lives and freedom in our relationships; we must become aware of the automatic functioning of our instincts and genetic programming. We must consider if we have the courage to override our instincts in order to make conscious decisions and responsible choices. This is how we can form relationships free of the subjugation and exploitation of women, as well as the emasculation and degradation of men.

As we become more aware of our natural responses we must not assume that our lower brains or instinctual behaviors have no function. We are beings with the ability to override these responses at times. On the contrary, our lower brains are very important when it comes to survival as individuals and as a species. The lower brain plays a crucial role when we are in a real life threatening situation or even when we fall in love. When a real emergency presents itself we have no time to think and make a conscious decision about what to do, such as jumping away from an oncoming car or pulling our hands away from a hot stove. These are managed by our instincts and you can see why. There is no time to think and process the information consciously. We must react immediately. The same thing happens when we fall in love, the most glorious of all the states of being. Nature has designed it that way so that we can make babies.

Unfortunately, we react immediately and without thinking when much less of an emergency occurs, i.e., a conversation where we perceive that we are or might be "emotionally hurt." Automatic reactions like these result more often in hurting ourselves and our relationships. So, when it comes to non life-threatening situations we should use our intuition and frontal lobe or neo-cortex to make our choices. In other words, we could think and formulate a response i.e., act responsibly instead of reacting automatically and instinctively.

Now that we have talked about our primitive origins of commitment, let's see what commitment is and why it is so important for a successful relationship. What does commitment mean to us as human beings at our present level of consciousness?

A quotation by W.H. Murray is widely misattributed to Johann Wolfgang von Goethe [1]. The following passage occurs near the beginning of Murray's The Scottish Himalayan Expedition (1951):

. . . But when I said that nothing had been done I erred in one important matter. We had definitely committed ourselves and were halfway out of our ruts. We had put down our passage money—booked a sailing to Bombay. This may sound too simple, but is great in consequence. Until one is committed, there is hesitancy, the chance to draw back, always ineffectiveness. Concerning all acts of initiative (and creation), there is one elementary truth the ignorance of which kills countless ideas and splendid plans: that the moment one definitely commits oneself, then providence moves, too. A whole stream of events issues from the decision, raising in one's favor all manner of unforeseen incidents, meetings and material assistance, which no man could have dreamt would have come his way. I learned a deep respect for one of Goethe's couplets:

"Whatever you can do or dream you can, begin it.

Boldness has genius, power and magic in it!"

W. H. Murray went on to conquer Mount Everest. His commitment was clear. That was the first big step to his success.

Strangely enough, our relationships sometimes look as if they present us with bigger obstacles than Mount Everest. People give up on their relationships ever so quickly at times. I think that one important missing component is a strong and real commitment to the relationship.

What is a commitment anyway? The dictionary says: *1. Devotion or dedication for example to a cause, person or relationship; 2. a planned arrangement or activity that cannot be avoided.*

In other words a commitment consists of an inner conviction and a public declaration of the context of future actions.

There is a difference between commitment to a person—which is loyalty—and a commitment to a relationship. Being committed to a relationship means that you are forming a unit. In a *Gameless Relationship* priorities shift from what "I want" to "what is best for us". This does not mean that you are going to sacrifice your needs. The word sacrifice is not even used in a healthy relationship because it implies martyrdom and lack of freedom, which in turn leads to blame and guilt. "Sacrifice" is a word used for manipulation, playing relationship games, and has no integrity in it.

Meeting one's needs is a prerogative of the relationship; therefore it is in both partners' best interest to cater to each other's needs. Of course, there is always the danger that one partner will overestimate or underestimate the importance of his/her own needs or the needs of the other. This may be done unintentionally, but if one is committed to the relationship, one will either self correct, or find a way to compromise if not able to do it alone. This is a matter of RESPONSIBILITY and INTEGRITY for both partners.

When people get married they exchange vows. In simple language, this means a *promise* or a *declaration*. Why is a marriage commitment so scary for so many people? Because it puts people outside of their comfort zone, and is a choice made with no experiential reference to the past. In fact, that's exactly what declaration is supposed to be. It's taking a risk into the big future, into unfamiliar and unknown territory, into a bigger and better future. Promise and declaration are probably two of the most important words and most powerful tools we have at our disposal for creating our relationship or any other area of our life successful and fulfilling.

How quickly we forget! About 50% of married couples forget what they promised, or consciously break their vows. That is the approximate percentage of divorces in this country. I wonder how many more people stay in unhappy relationships without ever getting divorced or breaking up.

The marriage ceremony is performed publicly in order that the vows cannot be broken easily. The whole pomp and circumstance is designed to give dignity, importance and lasting presence to the promises that are made. We invite people as guests to be present as witnesses to our promises who can keep us accountable and support us in keeping our word. That's the original idea.

Sadly, many weddings have become a display of material wealth, self-worth, ego or pride associated with the bride or groom's success in "catching" the other. A host of other things, which have nothing to do with the actual intention to keep the promise, have clouded the picture and the original intent has been lost. Guests often come to party, eat and drink well, forgetting, or not even being aware of their obligation and responsibility to the success of the relationship.

The friends and family at the ceremony are supposed to keep the bride and groom accountable for what they promised and to support them in fulfilling their promises. These are the real reasons for a wedding ceremony. The promises given at the marriage ceremony are certainly not the only ones that should be kept. A promise is our word given to another and to ourselves. It certainly does not mean that it may be broken easier than the marriage vows. As we will see later, this is a matter of honor and integrity.

By honoring our word as we honor ourselves we make sure that we stay together and that we take responsibility for our partner and our children. We know all too well that our biological instinct is not enough; without vows our children would often not have fathers and sometimes would be without mothers too. We would not need vows and marriage laws if we were by nature monogamous creatures. Unfortunately we are not. As we said, a marriage is a social agreement, whether formal or not, and in order to have families we need to make and keep certain promises.

That's how we succeed as humans: through language and honoring what we say. This is not a moral issue. This is more of an issue of development and evolution of the human species as well as the source of our own contentedness and happiness. It is much easier for us to grow when we are in a relationship and when our relationships are part of the community. Evolution has proved that we do better together than alone.

As stated earlier, women and men are different; they are two different types of the same species. They both have their natural strengths and weaknesses. That's why they function better together. They complement each other. In the future there may be some other arrangement that will work better than marriage. Although there are already some attempts in poly-amorous relationships, the results are mixed because they require highly conscious people with rigor, transparency, openness, integrity and trust. Only the strongest relationships with the highest commitment and integrity can survive multiple relationships. However, at the present time, monogamous relationships are still the norm in many cultures.

So, will being 100% committed to your relationship assure a *Gameless one*?

There are no 100% guarantees in life, because there is no such a thing. There is only "living" a day at a time. To live is a verb not a noun when it comes down to it. This applies to a relationship as well: It is about relating and it changes constantly from moment to moment. Every moment brings an opportunity, a challenge and temptation to change yourself to be different in the next moment.

Therefore, it is not so much about what you do or how you do it. Your actions, words, your listening, your interpretations, your thoughts and feelings all come from who you are being right now in every moment. Only you can make that choice. The future cannot be predicted; it can only be created. You always have a choice about what your future will look like by choosing who you will be *now*. Doing comes out of being—naturally, effortlessly. So, if you want tomorrow to be different than today, you have to be something different *today*. So, are you a person of integrity, or one without it? The choice is always yours. There is no middle ground.

Your responsibility in a *Gameless Relationship* is to keep the integrity of your commitment.

*Awareness Exercise: If you were to look at what you **do not want** in your life and consider that you are actually committed to constantly having it despite all your efforts to the contrary, how would you feel? Investigate how it is that you manage to keep it there even though you say that you do not want it. How do you deceive yourself? What conversations with yourself do you have to keep it in place? What beliefs are created out of these conversations? This question may sound strange, but what are you getting out of consistently having what you do not want? What is your pay-off for keeping it in place? And, most importantly, what does it cost you?*

*Now, think of the things that you **do want** in your life and already have. How did you get them? Was it due to your focus and constant attention? Did it come naturally to you, or did you have to put in a lot of effort? Was it pleasant or not? Can you see any **similarities** between the two?*

4. LOVE

Love is an underlying and all-encompassing principle and a support for the three other principles of a *Gameless Relationship*: Commitment, Integrity and Responsibility. Without love no *Gameless Relationship* can exist. Love is also the basis for not only a *Gameless Relationship*, but for life itself.

To Love Vs. Being In Love

There are two uses of the words "love" that often tend to be confused with one another, namely, *to love* and *to be in love, or to fall in love.*

Is being in love with a person and loving that person the same thing? Our language for the most part does not distinguish between the two, although there are similarities.

Some languages have many words for different kinds of loves. It is mostly differentiated by whom, or by what the love is bestowed upon. Sanskrit has about 90 different words for different kinds of love for different things, relations and relationships. We basically have very few: feeling, affection for, like, adoration, reverence, adulation, be keen on, worship, be devoted to, adore, have a weakness for, find irresistible and many more. Most of these words have a different primary meaning as well, and most of them refer to a feeling of being in love.

I would like to touch upon how to distinguish between being in love as opposed to loving someone. If we look closely we will first notice that one is a state of *being* and the other is an action, or *doing*. The first one is involuntary and the other is voluntary or intentional. In other words being in love is who you are, i.e. when you are in love it is a state of being.

On the other hand, when you love and express love, it becomes an actual conscious action, or doing. We often confuse the two, as in saying, "I love you" or "I do love you," but what we often mean is "I am in love with you." When we are in love, we just are. It is beyond our control, we have no choice. We "fall" in love, we do not voluntarily jump into it. We do not decide to be, or feel that way. We just are. We find ourselves in it.

You cannot find fault with a person with whom you are in love. It's a glorious feeling. For us there is no other way in which that that person *should* or *could* be.

We did not consciously decide to not notice their faults and shortcomings. For us, they do not have any. We are blind to what we do not want to see: love is blind. We are not open to reality. It's as if we're in a dream, not wanting to wake up. It is *that good.* In other words, we are convinced that the person we love is perfect in every way. This is not a conscious decision, it is an automatic belief, it is a given. We "know" the truth. This is the way things *are.* The person we are in love with is absolutely perfect in all respects. We see what we believe.

We are, after all, in love! This ability of ours to "blindly fall in love" is hardwired into humans. It certainly proved itself to be an effective component of the human reproductive process. But, being in love never lasts forever and many couples break up when they fall out of love. The usual reason given is, "I do not love you any more." Then someone wants to break up, only to find out that in future relationships, history repeats itself. They are seeking to recover that being-in-love high and as soon as it goes away again, so do they.

People do not seem to realize that falling out of love is ultimately inevitable. Life goes on, and ultimately we open our eyes to reality and start noticing that our partner is not "perfect." I am sure you have your own example of this. At last we start to believe what we see instead of vice versa. Many think that the only "true love" is the feeling you have when you are "madly in love." Couples don't even know that there is a much more rewarding and satisfying love to be had.

Real true love is love by choice. Not the one that you have no control over when you are mindlessly emerged in it and have no voice in when it will start or end. On the other hand, real "true love" is constantly self-generated. Being able to consciously generate love towards the other is nothing less than having the power to take control of your own life.

Unconditional Love, The Path To Freedom

To love, as opposed to being in love, is a conscious decision to *do* something: to love. It is an act of doing. It is an action to take—continuously. To consciously love means having no blind spots. It is a conscious choice in every moment to view and accept our "loved" ones *as being perfect exactly the way they are and being perfect exactly the way they are not.* Being in love includes only the first part of this statement, i.e. " . . . perfect exactly the way they are . . ." Unconditional love begins with an unconditional acceptance of who he/she is *and is not* right now.

This may sound a little odd. After all we all "know" that they are not always perfect especially when we realize there are differences between us. The only reason we may think that they are not perfect is because WE think that they *should* or *could* be someone else, behave differently, or be doing something else. Since our desires and expectations do not match up with who they are, or what they do, we think that they are WRONG, or that there is something WRONG with them. Also, we think they should be better or different.

Instead of looking at our partner and other people and blaming them for not being who and how *we* think they should be, we need to be aware of our tendency to create an imaginary reality about them. We have an idea of how things could be and a propensity to conclude that there is something wrong with what is actually happening right now. Then, if we catch ourselves in this process, we may realize that we have a choice.

Upon this choice our happiness and peace of mind rests: We can either accept our partners *as being perfect exactly the way they are and perfect exactly the way they are not,* or insist on living in the world of 'something is wrong' and continue to suffer. I understand that sometimes you wish he/she was different or better, but the starting point is to recognize and acknowledge that you cannot change him/her and to choose to accept the way he/she is NOW, at this moment. It does not mean that we cannot envision our partners to be much greater then they are willing to allow themselves to be, but that is a future issue. No one can be different then they are at the present moment, so you might just as well stop wishing for impossible and making yours and everyone else's life difficult.

They are dealing with their own lives the best way they know how and we can take the opportunity to understand them and/or accept them, to practice compassion and unconditional love, and give up the urge to control them. Unfortunately, we often take the behavior of our partner too personally. We think that the behavior of our partner has something to do with us. In the overwhelming majority of cases it is not about us.

Unconditional love, as the name implies, is love without conditions or reasons attached to it. You are either able to accept a person exactly the way she/he is, or you are not. Whenever you think that you love a person *because* of this or that, you are making it conditional, and conditions will change along the way. So love with attached conditions obviously cannot be unconditional. Whenever you attach a condition to loving someone there is a chance that the condition will cease to exist (like good looks or wealth).

This is another reason for a break up: people often think that "love" has magically disappeared, when, in fact, love has nothing to do with it. It was a "contract" in the first place. You, from the start, "loved" that person in exchange for the reason for which you said you loved him/her. That reason could have been infatuation, lust, or fulfilling some of your needs. When the reason disappeared, "love" did too.

Unconditional love, therefore, starts as the committed acceptance of your partner that underlies all healthy and happy relationships. This is the kind of love that I will be referring to in the future: the unconditional love, the foundation for all of the other principles of being in great relationships and having great lives.

I cannot emphasize enough, though, that loving someone unconditionally *does not mean* that you should live with, or even see the person if he/she has crossed your boundaries of physical or mental safety. You should never allow yourself to be physically or mentally abused. Be aware though: justifying undesired behaviors including our own is not love or compassion. It takes us out of integrity.

Unconditional love is one of the very highest places for which human spirituality always strives. To be in the space of unconditional love requires a commitment to our absolutely highest self. When you perceive the world around you as "perfect exactly the way it is and perfect exactly the way it is not," there is an enormous feeling of freedom and of somehow being invincible. In the presence of unconditional love, there is simply nothing to do, fix, or change. Everything seems to be just right, just as it should be. This does not mean that we will never attempt to create something different; it simply means that we give up fighting the reality of *what is*.

The games we play with ourselves are the games of "should," "would," and "could." These games are recipes for disaster in our relationships. I have heard the argument that unconditional love does not really exist and that humans are actually not capable of having it within themselves. I disagree.

Although I am aware of the difficulty of giving love unconditionally in every situation and in every moment, I know that when you do, you have peace, happiness and power permeating everywhere. There is a sense of absolute freedom, total lack of fear, and the knowledge that all is well and nothing is wrong. There is a certain sense of invincibility or certainty that nothing bad can happen to you. And it doesn't.

When you give acceptance to others, you show an enormous amount not only of love, but also respect, faith, support, compassion and appreciation simply for their existence. The reaction you get from others is also unique in itself. You'll find that others are willing to respect you and listen to your opinions and advice. In other words, everyone wants to be closer to you. You are loved. If you want to be loved, you must give love first. If you want to be accepted you must first accept yourself and others for who you and for who they are. Furthermore, if you want to be happy, you must first accept what IS, reality as it is . . . now.

So, if you want to have a *Gameless Relationship*, the first step is to accept your partner exactly the way she/he is and exactly the way he/she is not. Love is the basis for power and happiness

What Is Romance?

When a man does little things that say, "I care, I understand what you feel, I know what you like, I am happy to do things for you, and you are not alone," he is directly fulfilling a woman's need for romance. When a man does little things without a woman having to ask, she feels deeply loved. If he forgets to do them, though, a wise woman graciously persists in reminding him by asking for them in a non-demanding manner.

Romance for a woman is when a man does things without her having to ask.

A man receives love differently from a woman. He feels loved when she lets him know again and again that he is doing a good job of fulfilling her. Her good mood makes him feel loved. Even when she enjoys the weather, a part of him takes the credit. A man is happiest when a woman is fulfilled. While a woman feels romanced by flowers, chocolates, and planned dates, a man's sense of romance is fueled by a woman's appreciation of him. When he does little things for her and she appreciates it a lot, he feels most romantic.

Romance for a man is when a woman appreciates the things he does.

Women generally do not realize that what a man needs most is a loving message that he has fulfilled her. When she is happy about the things he provides for her, he feels loved. When he can do something for her, he lets in her love. The most important skill to have for showing love to a man is to catch him when he is doing something right and notice and appreciate him for it. The worst mistake is taking him for granted.

A man feels loved when he gets the message that he has made a difference, that he has been helpful in some way, and that his partner benefits from his presence. The other way to love a man is to minimize his mistakes whenever possible with statements like "It's no big deal" or "It's okay". Downplaying disappointments makes him much more open to future requests and needs.

When a man does things for a woman and she is fulfilled, they both win.

V. MAINTENANCE

CREATING SUPPORT

Humans are social beings. There is not much you can do on your own. The popular belief, especially in the western world, that we can succeed on our own is readily seen in the phrases that we admire, such as "He is a self-made man" or "I made it on my own" and "I did it myself." No one has ever done anything by themselves, short of dying. You will see the proof if you just look around. Are you alone in the world?

Life turned out the way it is because of the relationships we have had, starting with our mother without whom you would not be reading these pages. Parents always have the most influence on us whether we like it or not. We could not choose our parents, although we can now choose to choose them, but we certainly have a choice about whom we associate with in our adult lives.

FRIENDS

We mostly choose our friends from the people who seem to be the "same" as us, who like the things we like, share our views of the world and generally agree with us. These people become our friends. We never question their loyalty and their worth as friends; how much they contribute to our well being, or how much they stifle our development. We know that they support us in all of our endeavors. They believe everything we say and approve of all our actions. They are what we call our "best friends." They listen to all of our complaints about our "life dramas." They enjoy gossiping about other people and support our judgments and assessments never questioning us and readily endorsing our often-skewed picture of reality.

These so called "best friends" will always be on our side whenever we find any lame reason or excuse not to do what we promised, or not keep our commitments. They will never hold us accountable for our actions and will always find reasons and excuses for us if our own inventiveness stalls. However, they will be very quick to make us wrong if we do anything that does not support their view of how things are and their take on reality.

If you do something out of the "ordinary," something they do not expect from you, you may very quickly become an ex-friend. So, in order to keep such "best friends" you will often have to compromise your integrity, commitments and self-expression. You will have no chance of advancing in your development because you are always going to be held back and blackmailed with the "friendship" if you ever want to move on.

These are probably *not* the "best friends" that we want to have around for supporting us in our endeavors to be the best we can be and have the best relationships we want to have, such as *Gameless Relationships*. So, who do we want to be our friends? How do we choose them and what is so critical about having really good friends around us?

We have all had friends like the ones I described above when we were young. I have also mentioned the reasons we lost some of them whether we initiated it or not. We may still have such friends in our lives now. There is nothing wrong with that. They may very well be great people who mean well.

All we have to do is take responsibility for our actions around friends and family that are in this category. At the same time, we must create a circle of friends, acquaintances and colleagues around us that support us in what we are doing. Best friends are those who are willing to be committed to what we are committed to, help us stay the course, be our reality check, and accept us for who we are and who we are not. They will not judge us, or make us wrong, but will help us in our efforts to stay in integrity and be our best selves—always.

Your friends are the people who help you keep integrity in your relationship instead of siding with you every time something goes wrong and you blame your partner. Friends ask questions to help you make the right choices for yourself and open your eyes to reality.

Always look for friends who you can admire, who are in some areas better than you, from whom you can learn something and who can expand your vision of life. Friends are there to support you in your commitments. They are there to help you get up when you fall down and should neither feel sorry for you when you feel sorry for yourself, nor help you with justifications for your failure. They will hold you accountable for your actions and lovingly help you get back on track. Such people are your best friends. That's what it means to have powerful support from the people around you.

VI. FINDING FREEDOM

HOW TO PROSPER AND
BE JOYFULLY FREE

Freedom is the ability to express your highest self and to be at your best in a supportive environment.

If you ask most people what freedom is, they might say that freedom is the ability and permission to do whatever they want and whenever they want to do it. In other words, a life without responsibility and accountability for anything, and at the same time having unlimited free resources at our disposal. This is a rather infantile definition of freedom something that little Johnny would wish. And, I cannot blame little Johnny. He is a child to whom such a magical way of thinking is natural and appropriate.

The problem begins when we become adults and take an active role in forming relationships with others in today's society and get stuck with the attitudes of little Johnny. This is why many relationships do not work; none of the aspects of *Gameless Relationship* mentioned above are present in little Johnny's world.

— Without Integrity nothing works,
— Without Responsibility there is no personal or societal power,
— Without Commitment there is no creativity.

Without these three principles of a *Gameless Relationship* in little Jimmy's world, we would slide into entropy, chaos, and eventual extinction. And, last but not least, without Love there is no life. In order to be happy we need to create a move forward to fully express our talents with unbridled authenticity. Freedom is the ability to fulfill our potential as human beings. For most healthy humans that means helping forward the fulfillment of other people's dreams. We all have our own unique tools, abilities and talents by which we can achieve that, whether it is art, business, engineering, teaching, sports, or you name it. Whatever we take on, can be used to contribute to others, without exception. By contributing to others, we inevitably contribute even more to ourselves. Human society is an organic whole of which we are all a part and at the same time it makes us who we are. This environment provides us with the possibility and opportunity of being fully self-expressed.

If we insist on our own uniqueness and do *not* create *Gameless Relationships*, then we deny and stifle our development and happiness. Quite often we choose people in our relationships because they are in effect our psychic mirrors. This is because we need to learn something about ourselves by being in these particular relationships, even though we may not be aware of it.

We grow by learning to see our picture reflected back by the people with whom we are in relationship. This kind of learning is always challenging (mostly because of our resistance and illusions we have about who we are) and so, by default, relationships can require some work. We may even violently resist the knowledge offered to us. It takes an effort in self-awareness to recognize the inevitable gift our relationships bring to us. Avoiding responsibility for our relationships is avoiding the learning process of discovering who we are, what our purpose is, and our experience of happiness, personal fulfillment and freedom. Being in a *Gameless Relationship* creates a loving and supportive environment for the full expression of your life purpose, and realization of your dreams.

Awareness exercise. *At this point you may be a little suspicious, overwhelmed or cynical about this ever being possible for YOU. Maybe for some other people, but me!? You may think that this is an ideal that can never be reached. But, what is life without an ideal, without a dream? This may be an ideal that if pursued will bring the most dividends, including ongoing happiness and fulfillment. Isn't that what we all want? Well, I invite you not to get discouraged. And here is why: this is a path, a process. This is not somewhere to be, at the top of the mountain, to reach the goal of a Gameless Relationship. As we said before, a relationship is not a noun it is a verb; to relate. Therefore, any relationship is constantly happening, in day-to-day relating. This is when happiness is found, NOW!*

I invite you to start noticing when any of the principles (Integrity, Responsibility, Commitment and Love) are missing when you are relating to anyone and then:

— Identify which one of the four is missing.
— Notice how resistant you are about putting it in place
— Recognize that you *are* getting something out of not having it present.
— What does it ultimately cost you?
— What is the gain/cost ratio?
— What would it take for you to put it in place?

You may decide to write all this down or to just make a mental note. However you decide to proceed, start becoming aware of your power to create any kind of relationship that you want. In fact, you are already doing it; YOU HAVE THE RELATIONSHIP THAT YOU WANT TO HAVE. By the same token, you can have any relationship you want, even a *Gameless Relationship*. All you have to do is create the relationship you want. The question is: *What do you want?*

As you can see, *Gameless Relationships* are contexts in which we are able to fully express ourselves, pursue our dreams, and have complete support from our environment.

VII. BE A LEADER

LET OTHERS SEEK YOU
FOR YOUR WISDOM

Leadership is the willingness to be a cause in the matter and keep the highest standards present for others.

I think that by now you are clear that putting the four principles into everyday practice would start building your credibility with the people around you. Your sense of purpose, love, integrity, happiness and ease of dealing with challenges will start becoming apparent to everyone you have a relationship with, from your business partner to the cashier at the local market. People will start looking up to you.

Not only will you become a respected member of your community, but you will also be able to influence the way your community develops. You will not only have a voice in the substance of your own life, but also in the dealings of the community at large, but only if you choose to do so. You will be a bona fide leader.

I am sure that now you have already noticed that this is not solely a guide to how to achieve *The Gameless Relationship,* but that there is more to it. It is also a developmental strategy for winning the game of life.

As I end this book, I thank you and acknowledge you for your courage and willingness to be confronted by and deal with what did not work in your life.

The time to step off the bleachers and onto the court is NOW. This action will mostly consist of not yet completed conversations as well as the ones yet to be had. *The Gameles Relationship* is not a given. It requires an investment of energy that goes in conversations, which sometimes are not comfortable but are always committed, responsible and loving. Keep in mind that your relationship is as good as your last conversation. Treat every conversation as an expression of an ideal relationship, *The Gameless Relationship*. 100% is a magical number. Strive for it in your integrity, with your responsibilities and with your commitments.

Never let dust collect on this or similar books. Keep them handy until the *four principles: Integrity, Responsibility, Commitment and Love* become your second nature—or first one, for that matter.

FURTHER RECOMMENDED READING AND EDUCATION

This is some of the material I find helpful and insightful.

Re-create Your Life: Transforming Yourself and Your World
by Morty Lefkoe
The Last Word on Power
by Tracy Goss
The Power of Now: A Guide to Spiritual Enlightenment
by Eckhart Tolle
Spiral Dynamics: Mastering Values, Leadership and Change
by Don Edward Beck and Christopher Cowan
Big Mind—Big Heart: Finding Your Way
by Dennis Genpo Merzel
All works
by Ken Wilber
The Evolving Self
by Mihaly Csikszentmihalyi
The Three Laws of Performance
by Steve Zafron and Dave Logan

http://www.thework.com/index.asp
  Experiencing the reality. Powerful and SIMPLE
http://www.understandmen.com/
  The best course out there for women only
http://www.understandmen.com/understandingwomen/index.html
  Ditto. For men and women
http://www.rie.org/
  This is how we should have started out. For babies, mothers and fathers
http://www.abraham-hicks.com/
  Creating our lives
http://www.fieldcenter.org/
  Ditto
http://www.immrama.org/brainwave/brainwave.html
  Meditation CDs—the best!
http://www.landmarkeducation.com/
  Awesome course!

I am eternally grateful to my parents, my wife Antoinette, my daughter Diana, and all the teachers, mentors and coaches, as well as my readers and participants in my courses throughout my learning, growing and evolving process. You will always be in my thoughts and in my heart.